D.E.R.O.S.

A Collection of Post-traumatic Poetry

by
Charlie-2

To Mark
Pleasure to know you
Good Luck to JP !

Sincerely

Charlie 2

1st Edition
Plastic Spoon Press

Plastic Spoon Press
P.O. Box 24156, Lansing, MI 48909-4156

Printed in the United States of America

1st Edition

Printing: 1 2 3 4 5 6 7 8 9 10
Year: 7 8 9 0 1 2 3 4 5 6

Library of Congress Catalog Number 88-082261

Charlie-2
D.E.R.O.S.
Post-traumatic Poetry

ISBN 0-9657424-0-7

Cover design by Daniel P. Ryan

From the Author

During my time in Vietnam, I worked with the 5th Group (Special Forces), the 1st Infantry Division, and the 173rd Airborne Brigade as a young officer. I lost almost all of my commissioning class of 218 men and the rest have been dying off since. I am the last one alive, effective date 14 Dec 87. I consider that living, being the last one alive, was not pure luck.

I am a living example of what war can do to someone in the extreme. I am alive through chemistry and the wonders of the Almighty. My extraordinarily well developed survivor's instinct, unfortunately, prevents suicide. In Vietnam, I had enormous control over life and death, indiscriminantly, with full authority. I came back, highly decorated and looking like a Christmas tree, to my Country's scorn and ridicule. It took its toll.

I pay the price of living every moment of every day in agony and guilt - I'm still fighting in Vietnam. I have PTSD, Post-traumatic Stress Disorder, rated at 100% disability by the Veterans' Administration. It began in 1972 and has been with me ever since. I am forced to take large (prescribed) quantities of serious psychotropic medications just to keep me reasonably functional and these are taking their toll on my physical condition.

My only means of communication are writing and talking on the telephone. Otherwise, I am isolated. I've had no friends since 1969. No one wanted a mixed-up vet back then, eighteen years ago. Even my family disowned me. My car, a Triumph Spitfire, was my home for three years. The V.A. said, "Don't worry. The nightmares and flashbacks will go away." They never did. After 17 admissions to VA Hospitals, they finally asked me about my military history. They had refused to listen before.

In Vietnam, the officers and men, who saw extensive combat, had to totally block out any and every emotion in order to survive. We developed a numbing response, which is actually no response at all, emotional or sensorial. Without this ability to block out, we would eventually be killed through negligence or self-destruction.

Then, there was Hanoi Jane. She killed more men by changing their drive to win to "I'd rather quit" and soon enough... death due to fatal errors in judgement! Newspaper clippings from home and, of course, Dear John letters further destroyed morale. <u>And the rest of the good folks at home changed channels instead of policies</u>. Vietnam veterans returned home to "Baby Killer!" and to spittle, and piss-filled water balloons, and various other forms of "Thank You." Needless to say, we retained our numbness.

In 1978, years too late for some, the Veterans Administration finally admitted I and others like me had a "problem." They gave it the name, "Post-traumatic Stress Disorder," and began treatment in 1980.

I call my work "Post-traumatic Poetry." It is purposely devoid of emotion and sensory detail because that is the way it happened. Some of it has been used for therapy by myself and the other vets who have read it. God willing, it will help other vets, their families, friends, and help the younger generation understand what really happened in Vietnam - the truth, this time.

Charlie-2

Dedication

I dedicate this book to Robert X. Ryan, the finest fellow combat officer I have ever known (He died Dec. 1987.), to his very caring and loving wife, Bonnie, and to Bob's family, for giving me, as I grew up, a role model to follow, his happily married parents. Bless you.

I can never leave out my wife, for without her saving my life, putting the pieces of my thoughts in order, you would not be reading this. Her intestinal fortitude is beyond my belief. She is my wife, editor, secretary, and "cheering section," and one hell of a Lady. Thanks, Honey.

Special Thanks

To Vietnam, for the "delightful" experience,

To all the nurses in Vietnam! Thanks, Kathy Tribble,

To my OCS Co. Sorry you couldn't make it to the reunion,

To Jerry Carmichael, for being the first to realize I had PTSD,

To Sarah Haley, LICSW, for starting me on correct therapy,

To Nancy McKee, Dr. Chamberlain, and all the others who help with my therapy,

To Rosanne, Barb and Kathy, for helping us keep our family together,

To Everyone who helped us when we needed it so badly,

And a very special thanks to Josh Blackmore for helping this book become a reality.

Thanks, so much!
Charlie-2

A special "thanks for nothing" to all those people who never listened and you know who you are.

D.E.R.O.S.

Remember the old saying of the '60's,
"Suppose they gave a war and nobody came?"
Try this . . .
They gave a war and nobody cared.

Job Description

Wanted: one young man who can out-shoot, out-think, outwit both his adversary and also the personnel that are in his charge.

Must have working knowledge of psychiatry, psychology, medicine, social work, priesthood, and public relations. Must have the wisdom of a Supreme Court Justice and the tenacity of a pirrhana. Must have unlimited compassion for his men but never show it, and yet, at the same time, be able to condemn them to death. Must be wise, and have the ability to write: "Dear Mr. and Mrs. _____Your son was a great man, not just a great soldier. Feel proud of your son, as I am. He died doing what he did best, serving his Country. We miss him and we loved him."

Anyone interested in this occupation must be evaluated by a former combat officer, who made it out alive. This occupation is not for one who expects reward or fears death. It is solely for the individual who can give constantly and receive a can or two of peaches for his job well done. Or a smile from a soldier placed on a medivac chopper, dying.

Even when the worst has begun and it may go one way or the other. Death is imminent. You look at your men and say "no supplies, no food, water, ammunition, mail. 'Too dangerous to attempt.' The boss wants to know if we can hold on for awhile." You look again at your men, not knowing exactly what to expect. They give you thumbs up. "Sir, next time get us cherry KoolAid."

I can't see for the life of me who wouldn't want this job.

(2LT) Army, INF

1

D.E.R.O.S.

The day we got our commissions, no one had a peep to say
to each other. We had in our possession our orders to proceed
to further training upon completion.

To USAPAC - RVN. VIETNAM.

THE CONG . . . THE HEAT . . .THE RAIN . . .

THE BLOOD . . . THE LIVING, THE DEAD . . .

THE HAVES AND HAVE NOTS . . .

THE BITS, THE PIECES . . . THE BOOBY TRAPS

AND THE BODY BAGS, BAGS, BAGS . . .

THE REPLACEMENTS . . .

AND YOUR REPLACEMENT, SOMEWHERE ON HIS WAY.

DON'T HURRY FOR MY SAKE, PAL. I CAN WAIT TILL

D.E.R.O.S.!—

DATE EXPECTED TO RETURN FROM OVER SEAS.

Note the word *"expected."* . . . .
Why did they have to put that in?

OCS Co.

My God, we were great!
So anxious to get to the war
with a seething compulsive desire
to take hold, take command,
and leap into glory.

But the blinders and ear plugs
we were wearing during OCS -
Officer Candidate School -
were not GI issue in Viet Nam.
The weapons fired live ammo.

The blood was real and sticky
and the first time you wore the body parts
of the man in front of you,
splinters of bone in your face,
you knew . . . it would happen again.

School Friends

In college, my friends and I,
  eight of us,
  shared an apartment,
  assuming that 80-90%
  would at least be in contact
  on occasion, after graduation,
  sometime in our lives.

In the Army,
  "Take any school" -

Flight school, here we were,
  happy to be qualified
  to learn to fly.

At that time we didn't think
  that failure meant success, living, coming home
  carrying a bag,
  not in one.

Special Forces -
  No comment.
  Same concept.

Accepting a commission in the Infantry,
  topping it off with teaching ROTC guys
  to kill,

And then, for spice,
    just add the paratroops,
    jungle operations, warfare,
    can't forget Ranger School.

And last, but not least,
    flying on a one way ticket.

Officers provided their own transportation
    up to Hawaii or Japan.
    The ticket agent said,
    "All military are one way.
    Standby or booked."

Ironic -
    They should have sold round trip -
    made some extra money.

All those schools were not there to make friends
    but rather good memories
    or pallbearers.

Making friends was not a problem.
    Keeping them was.

"Deliver Us From Evil"

The soft breath of life
    carried no distance to my ear.
    I have lost three with one rocket.

All that covers me now
    is the mingling of bloods
    and the crackling of the dried

Sticking to my face,
    splintered bone
    layered on me
    like first snow hides the past
    proper disguise for useless death

I slowly slide between the missing body parts
    for I.D. tags
    and pocket them, leaving one
    properly attached to the largest
    identifiable body part.

I want to salvage what I can
    of their heroic lives
    before Graves Registration
    changes names to numbers

and sends all personal effects
    without discretion
    to the "last known address."

        "Taps" -

    (the blockout phase)

I'll miss these men.
    They were all of eighteen.

I swallow my grief
    and go on, dear Lord,
Numb as numb can be!

Tit for Tat

Death
   through the eyes of my own soldiers
   and my own,
   from the eyes of my enemy
   when they were my friends
   during the day.
   The enemy that we killed
   were young, old, male, female,
   all out to do us in.
   That, we knew.

All the while we were both on
   different sides,
   we always knew
   we were not on equal terms.
   But we still gave them food
   and medical attention.
   We had hopes that Vietnam would be
   one great country someday.

Checking My Daytime Friends

I suppose the most difficult assignment I encountered
   was that of a visitor
   using CIDG and locals for my purpose.

The object was to locate,
   through old means - fear,
   (torture was out)
   to ascertain locations,
   numbers, names, etc.,
   of the V.C. leaders,
   many of the village chiefs,
   north to south,
   north of Ban Me Thout.

It worked this way -
   the Vietnamese were threatened
   by the Viet Cong
   with their lives
   if they would not cooperate.
   The chief would be slaughtered
   in front of his family.
   Removal of exterior organs while still alive
   was quite common.

I had the same duties,
   to gather information on the V.C.
   and if they cooperated,
   we would relocate the entire village
   to a safe area,
   but my methods were not as crude.
   Most of these villages were hard-core.

I would tell my interpreter
   to ask three simple questions
   of which I knew the answers.
   When they were correct, nothing happened.
   When they withheld info,
   I took them outside the village,
   fired once in the air,
   came back, asked the same.
   Nothing?
   I asked again.
   This time, one well-placed round was fired.
   Then we left.
   On to another V.C. village.

Difficult

Soldiers gather together
   after a battle
   around their dead,
   for consolation,
   and a form of ceremony.

Most of these gatherings
   are impossible to tell you about -
   you're not invited -
   and I know why.

It hurt very much!
   But for me
   to break their sacred barrier
   was "no way."

It was my job
   to tag and identify only - (somewhat).
   always keep your distance -
   don't turn your back for awhile.

You orchestrated it!

Just Business

When I lost a fellow officer,
   it was a message - short and sweet-
   "Charlie 4. The LT - Wiped."

And all I could do was
   "Roger, thanks much. Out."

This bothers me
   even today as I write.

A commission is not the most enviable thing to have.
   In war, it's death.
   In peace time, it's paperwork.
   But you are the one
   who will take the fall.

To a combat officer,
   death is a natural progression.

More Than Strays

When you're tightly wrapped,
   Your "shit in order,"
   The Man has spoken!
   Pucker factor waiting to blow,
   CHARLIE'S COMING THROUGH.

New bananas packed full.
   Favorite frag bag loaded.
   Starlight has the juice.
   All freq's memorized
   on the palm of your left hand.

The mission is
   Don't come back empty,
   except your basic load.
   "Have I ever let you down?"
   LTC - "No comment."

Charlie is almost here!
   Not yet.
   You smell first,
   just before you hear.
   And then you see.

Higher says, some strays from the hills.
   (200 men, by division standards, are strays.)
   Bull shit! Bull shit!
   You know inside, deep inside
   'cause tomorrow is body-count day.
   And you hope you will be the one
   to call them in.

The Man says
  can't get any air or ground support.
  Can't let Charlie know
  we've got them by the balls.
  So, now it's up to the eighteen of us
  And they're two hundred plus.

I take the handset of the PRC 25,
  and like a DJ -
  "It's 0145 hours, folks.
  The only live station on the air.
  I'll be with you most of the night.
  Keep your powder dry, boys,
  and we'll make it through the night!"

Battalion calls back
  "Stop broadcasting!"
  "Roger that. Out."
  "Far out!" I say to myself.

0400 hrs. Shit! There's Charlie.
  Holy Christ, that's a fuckin' battalion!
  "60's, switch to non-tracers."
  "Roger."
  "Mornin', Charlie," I whisper.
  "OK, boys. Do it 'til it stops! - FIRE!"

The screaming starts
  just before they fall to grace -
  all night long
  the barrels on the 60's glow orange.
  Body count is like your first lay
  and your last goodbye.

You discover that you can raise your status -
   no prisoners,
   just overkill the gooks
   and yell, "fire in the hole!"
   Search for info
   and trade the weapons to the REMF's
   so they go home heroes
   and your men, a little wealthier.

When the count is done,
   yours are either bagged, medivaced, -
   or having breakfast
   and looking like the bag
   is their only way home.

This day the Brass wants to share with us
   the victory.
   The General Staff shows up - I like him.
   I answer only his questions.
   He asks the right kind.
   If you get a medal,
   it's mostly posthumously.

I watch him walk over the scene
   and where I first blew the bush.
   He isn't a macho General.
   He's a caring, grandfather-type.
   As he steps over the god-awful mess,
   I know he is praying silently.

We walk together.
    Yes, I am ten feet tall
    and rubber-legged.
    "Heard you were in the delivery business also.
    I think what you did from 0130 'til now,
    how hard it is,
    and you cover with, 'No problem, Sir!'
    Did you know that your men,
    every chance they have,
    want you to be awarded?
    Take them! They are proud!"

"Sir, they just want me out of the field
    to stick me with the REMF's for awhile."
    He chuckled
    as though it had happened to him
    - years ago.

Nice Night

Oh, God, this night was beautiful,
   Warm and kind.
   The stars were
   on our side.

We just laid back
   and thought not of war
   or who was going to die
   before the sun was up.

But of very common things
   like "Why does the grass at home
   need cutting all the time
   and here it never does?"

We never grew anything over here.
   Maybe we should have.

The soil was rich, lots of minerals,
   Deposits from the air.
   Bone meal, for fertilizer.
   And rain, plenty of rain.

Next time I join a war,
   I'll bring some seed
   and see if something good will grow.

Viet Nam '69

Killing hot,
   the heat of the writhing bodies
   still sweating
   and you wait
   for that last reach for life.

You don't want anyone to touch you, talk to you,
   interrupt your rapport with the dying.

It is a very private moment,
   as though you are awaiting a transformation,
   a rebirth before your eyes.

But it usually ends with a whimper
   and it's very, very close.

            And then you pray.

After Action Report

I see the flash, mortars.
　　We get closer,
　　looks like a Stone Age picnic,
　　hunting for the beast
　　at the end of the tunnel.

You recognize this man with his son
　　and a girl handing the mortar rounds
　　to her brother.

I wish I could forget tonight.

Time, 4 a.m.
　　12 Jan 1970
　　3 KIA.
　　1 mortar tube.
　　No remaining rounds.
　　Negative further.
　　Charlie-2, out!

. . . Doesn't anyone want to know their names?

The Medivac

LZ . . . Hot as hell. No stars.
  Tap door gunner –
  "Find out how many
  we have picked up."

"Roger. Eighteen, Sir."
  "Shit." Missing two.

"I need a short sweep."
  Pilot rogers me thumbs up.

I jumped into the darkness.
  Two dead – get tags.
  Still taking fire.
  Up into that black night
  like ravens we flee.

"Battalion wants info, now,
  before attempt to 93rd EVAC."
  "Fuck 'em! Tell them
  I have four extremely dying
  and three to four extremely next."
  Thumbs up.

"Black Cat,
  I thought we "Idiot Sticks"
  were wacked."

1969

Dear Folks,

What the papers say at home
   don't tell the whole story.

Yesterday, I killed two little ones.
   In your papers, or on the news,
   that's all it would tell.

Those two little ones
   fragged one of my squads,
   killed four,
   while we were giving them our C-rations
   and some basic medical treatment.

Does that change your mind?

Not really.

Every day, I get closer to my time to come home.
   But I don't want to come back to my "home."
   I don't think you even care
   if I do or not.

In fact, I'm ashamed
   of my country's half-truths
   or outright lies
   and you buy it.

This place is more like home.
   You can tell who the enemy is
   most of the time.

But back in your country
   I'm being betrayed.

Don't condemn me!
   Condemn war!

OK

One thing I remember about the fighting . . .
   There's not too much said before.
   The fear is just settling in
   and the mind and body are becoming one.

Now it happens. You're engaged in combat.
   The firing is in a frenzy.
   Constant, constant, - no slowing down.
   Death all around.
   Screaming. Screaming.
   "Shut up!" you say to yourself.
   You hope it will end soon.

Then there is quiet . . .
   Eerie . . . Motionless . . .
   Screaming has stopped dead!

Then, as though nothing had happened,
   you hear in the darkness,
   "Who the fuck stole my toothbrush?"

And even you stop to think,
   "Gee, I wonder who would do a thing like that!"

You forget the war for a second.
   Your mind does one thing,
   your body another.

ARVN Ambush Technique - 1970

I awake, cold,
   a rancid mist surrounding me.
   I close my eyes and realize
   they are already closed.

I open them and see some light.
   I smell wax, taste salt.
   my mouth is filled with vomit.
   My body does not respond to the taste.
   I am only responding with my eyes.

Imbedded in my mind is "Freeze -
   Use senses first.
   No movement."
   Survival.

Focus my eyes
   on this guy beside me.
   Who is it? ARVN? - yes.
   Assholes slept through it -
   None of these are mine!

Don't move, wait!
   Get the puke out.
   I look at it - Clotted blood, shit!
   Internal hemorrhage?
   Where? I don't feel sick.

Ignore pain, don't respond.
   Good training.
   Try and tell yourself
   you want pain where the problem is
   without moving any voluntary muscles.

Time elapsed - ten minutes? ten seconds?
   I smell something different,
   the smell I don't want.
   It's Victor Charles'.
   My God, my senses are good.

I hear movement, no voices.
   Someone leaving the scene.
   The smell is all wrong
   for what should be all right.
   Holy shit. What happened?
   I was hoping for a nightmare
   and found that it was real!

More movement - quick steps.
   Still no voices. What the fuck?
   Now I feel the pain, in my mouth.
   It's about time, I say to myself.
   Maybe it's not internal bleeding.

Time elapsed - one minute? an hour?
   Another nightmare?
   Maybe I'm dead!

If this is dead, it sure isn't boring
   except that I can't move.
   All I know is death is all around me.
   But who is moving?

OK, movement has stopped.
   Get it ready,
   right hand, thumb - feel
   safety is off.
   Put it on Rock & Roll, one click up.
   OK, let's see what we have here.
   All I gotta do is jump up, fire away,
   and hope God knows I'm here.

Just then,
   somebody rolls me over on my back.
   I close my eyes - Possum Time.
   Whoever it is is gonna be dead.

"Jesus Christ, this LT is alive!"

   No shit, Sherlock!

Think About It

Someone found some rope "hemp."
   We strung it over a branch
   that went ten feet from the shore
   into the river.

We played this for a few hours.
   It was not the rainy season.
   It was good and wet.
   We were children once again.

The fun played tricks on us -
   We were truly happy!
   Our security, fine.

A scream!
   Several screams!!!
   Some men felt pulled under
   by their own men,
   But they weren't!

Later they were found
   tied by their ankles
   to some old limbs
   just ten or more feet
   from the safety
   of our hands.

      . . . Ever feel hopeless?

Sweet Spot

I remember kneeling
  beside this fallen foe,
  not sure that it was I that hit him,
  but most likely me.

It was the sweet spot
  that I always aimed for.
  "Sweet spot" in golf - a firm hit
  for longer distance.

My sweet spot was the belly.
  Enemy would drop faster
  and usually present me
  with another one right behind.
  Somewhat like bowling.

This one wasn't kicking.
  He was losing quickly,
  I think, painlessly.

This I don't understand -
  He looked at me as if I were his friend.
  I was the last face he would see.

Maybe that's it.
  Maybe he just made peace with me
  In his soul

Then, I did something I had never done.
  I wrapped his wounds
  with my only bandage.

It did no earthly good
   at least, not for me.

That night, around 3 or 4 a.m.,
   we heard them come
   for the other bodies.
   My interpretor said that they were talking
   about how some people are still good.

I started carrying more bandages.
   They made good sweat bands.
   And a way of saying
   There is still love on earth.

Embarrassed, To Say The Least.

One rainy night, I was moving up to the point.
   I felt this boot in my face,
   so I moved to his right side,
   couldn't hear or see shit five inches away.
   Monsoon time.

As usual, I started a quiet monologue.
   He didn't say much.
   I told him I was Charlie-2.
   Where was Charlie-3?
   He shrugged his shoulders,
   as if to say, "I don't know."
   This kind of communication was quite common.

Finally, the sun rose.
   I rolled over, sat up, and picked up the hand set,
   called in my location,
   the answer I got said, "You can't be!
   We're on the south side of the river,
   back about 100 meters in the woodline."

I looked back and saw the river.
   "Looks like we're both lost!
   I'll cover for you. –

"Charlie-3, Charlie3, Charlie-2, over.
   Charlie-3. Charlie-2.
   I've got one of yours with me.
   What? You have everyone there?
   Who the fuck is this......?

I rolled him over –
   died during the night.

I often wonder if I drove him to his death
   with my constant mouthing off.
   I don't think he understood what I said.

He was my enemy –
   the one they left behind.
   Thanks again, Lord.

Something Like The Movies

I had this new kid about one week.
   No legs. He couldn't see or move.
   I said, "Looking good, Troop."
   "Thank you, Sir!
   Am I going to die?"

I said, "Not before I do."
   "For real?"
   "Well, let's put it this way -
   when you have had your first child
   and it's a boy, (chopper was ready)
   name him after me."
   "Yes, sir," he said.

I kept a strong face
   until he took off.
   Visiting day, nurse said
   Lost too much of him.

His letter to his Honey,
   wife or girl -
   "Let's have a baby boy
   and call him Charlie-2.
   That's what my LT's name is."

"I think he was serious," the nurse said.
   He went to Japan and died.
   The letter went in the mailbox to his...

We never knew.

Man's Best Friend, By Far

I once had a dog named after me,
   "Charlie-2"
   I carried him on top of my rucksack.
   We used him on ambush at night
   and he saved our hides many times.

His stomach would rumble
   when the gooks were near
   and he'd growl when it was time
   to blow the bush.
   He was great!

I guess he figured he owed us one,
   considering that he would have been
   a nice meal for them,
   if we hadn't gotten to him first.

Getting Caught!

I had this one guy
   whose wife would send him Polaroids.
   - It really wasn't fair.
   The poor guy
   looked like he had an umbrella in his pocket
   most of the time.

The thing that bothered me was during the night,
   Off in the distance, you'd hear noises
   like "slapping a hollow chicken."

I knew it was him!
   Because even in the rain,
   it didn't remove the stain.
   How poetic.

I couldn't tell him to stop
   because once you start,
   you really don't want to stop.
   So I would pass it on to him verbally,
   man to man, in a whisper -

      "Hurry up."
But by the time it got to him,
   it was all over anyway,
      "literally."

I even thought of giving him a direct order to stop,
   telling him to stop, or his wife to stop,
   or whatever.

So, the following day, I called him over
   and said, "I don't need to hear this racket.
   So help me, I'll cut it off."

I meant his mail.
   He thought I meant something else.

Essence

The essence of Viet Nam
   cannot be captured on film,
   described, or learned from books.

Neither time nor memories can change
   the meaning of its past -
   what it meant to each of us.

It was a star-studded sky,
   filled with mystery,
   intrigue.

Every hidden weapon used against us
   was a peacock in full regalia,
   thousands of hidden eyes
   behind each leaf.

The one that took your life
   was most on your mind.
   Getting bagged and tagged wasn't.

Phenix

The forbidding glance
at your fiance's picture.
You have just wasted hours, maybe days,
of psychological preparation,
preparing your own brand
of annihilation -
You know -
the kind that never creeps back
to upset your other styles of murder.
You know.
The ones you can blame on the enemy.

Hello

One day the mail came.
   It was two weeks late
   but it didn't matter to me.
   All my letters were numbered.
   But this batch had a tape,
   sides one and two.

A few weeks later,
   I had the use of a tape player
   in the Rear.

We were bringing five bodies back for shipment
   and the guy at Graves Registration
   had a tape deck right there.
   Great!
   This tape should help my morale.

It was from my fiance.
   She changed my name to John.

. . . She always had great timing.

These Things Happen

3 a.m.
   I found a small book of notes
   without a single hole
   from the Claymore.

I gave it to my interpretor
   when I got back.

He read,
   "My love,
   the country will be one.
   We will live here.
   The land is rich.
   It will be, my love,
   our new homeland."

The only info I could retrieve without light
   was this book.

It went forward,
   along with the three soldiers' bodies
   at first light.

Three days later, I was told
   one of the three was six months pregnant.
   None of the others were.
   But all the soldiers were ammo bearers only.
   "Nothing important."

Australian Rules

I remember a special day in 1970.
 It was RAINING.
 The mud was almost knee deep,
 everyone was hungry,
 and we had just gotten back
 after thirty days
 of Typical Tropical Shit (combat.)

We were offered a hot meal.
 "Thanks anyway, Sir,
 but we have already made plans."
 We played mudball.

The people in the Rear,
 with sandbagged hootches,
 mattresses, TV's,
 radios, real food,
 and water you could see through,
 could not understand.
 We never expected them to,
 so why even try to explain.

That afternoon,
 we went out again.
 We came back days later
 needing more bodies
 and a pick-up game
 before moving out.

R & R, July '70

It's not hard to remember the 4th of July.
   I spent it in Hawaii.
   It was the worst 4th ever.

Everything about it wasn't right
   except the water.
   It tasted fantastic!

I had to get back to Vietnam - ASAP.
   How were the men?
   Were they in the Rear, as ordered,
   till I get back?

I sent them all postcards
   wishing I was there.

During the third day,
   Nixon categorically denied
   Cambodia intervention.

I told her something had come up.
   (We'd been there forever.)
   I had to get back.
   She didn't understand.
   I didn't understand either,
   until now.

Day After Day

"Kent - hit!
    Two others! Can't tell."
    At 4 a.m., we were hit again.

What the hell was that?
    I picked up two heads from the inside.
    I could see shit in front of me.
    Blood in my eyes.
    That's all I could smell -
    Sixty feet of shit.

Who were these two?
    Must be us - don't smell fishy.
    That was all I could find of them
    So we flipped a coin -
    Who was who.
    Sorry, guys, but you know who you are
    And that's what counts.

I said that to them
    and Kent on the chopper lifts off.
    "Hey, Sir!
    My hand cupped my ear, "What?"

"Nobody will call me 'asshole' ever again."
    I smiled. "Right." Thumbs up.
    He won't piss standing up again either,
    Under my breath.

The New Guy

You watch this kid
    Fire fight after fire fight.

You hope he isn't wasted
    because you don't even know his name
    and he's been with you for two months.

He gets no mail to identify him
    and I'm too damned embarrassed to ask.

So you think,
    "If I get it before he does,
    no problem,
    no embarrassment."

These are called rest breaks
    for your mind.

John

A friend of mine
  played for both sides.
  He was my interpreter.

We got along great.
  He was lots of fun to be with.

He would talk about the University
  in Hanoi
  where he graduated.

I trusted him
  with my life.

One day,
  an American came to see me
  and told me all about him.

I asked if I could give him over
  to the South Vietnamese.
  No go.
  How about a trade with the North?
  No go.

I went to him and told him
  what I was told.
  He said it was true.
  Why?
  To stay alive.

The American told me
  what I would have to do.

John came over to me.
  We both smiled, shook hands.
  He knew.
  He turned.

  I fired.

Goodbye, John.

Just Not Fair

I remember the feeling of this soldier's life
   just rushing out of him.
   He was saying, "It's not fair! It's just not fair!"
   I said, "Take it easy. You'll be fine."
   you're right. It isn't fair - to anyone.

A week later, I went to make the rounds,
   visit the guys at the 93rd EVAC.
   He died before I got there.

The nurse asked me if he had problems at home.
   I said, "I don't think so."
   She said, "I can't go through his personal effects.
   I suppose you can do anything that you want."
   "Why?"
   "Last night, he pulled the IV's out
   and bled himself into the mattress."

I got his bag, looked through it,
   found some letters and pocketed them.
   I told her, "You didn't see that!"

His fiance wrote -
   she did not want to marry a man
   who would kill women and children
   and old men and women.

The next letter was even better -
   ONTARIO, CANADA -
   a picture of her and a friend of his.

I think back -
   What did he mean by "not fair?"

43

Dad, Others Get Cookies

One Day The Mail Came In A Box
   This particular day was not ordinary.
   It started with rations, mail, a new man or two,
   and water - what the fuck - no water?
   Shiiiiit!
   (They put it in 3 plastic bags, drop it,
   and hope it will survive the fall.)
   What the fuck are they doing?

That's when we discovered a new source of water!
   Bomb crater water,
   like green Wheatina,
   not to forget the "water purification tablet"
   with a little tab inside the bottle
   which read, "Do not eat."
   What did they think we were? Marines?
   And boy, did they taste bitter!

I got a package from S.S. Pierce,
   a very well known establishment for the wealthy gourmet.
   My Dad sent smoked clams in a can,
   knakworst, olives, black and green, cocktail onions,
   escargot, with the shells in plastic on top of the can.

Before I could say, "Stop,"
   my RTO was yelling at the top of his lungs,
   "Charlie-2 can't get us water
   but he gets steamed clams and cocktail shrimp."
   "Hey, LT, who's it from?"
   "The Salvation Army," I said.

Goodbye - by the Late Clayton

I was sitting there in the rain,
   thinking of Debbie Reynolds and Donald O'Connor
   dancing in the rain.
   Clayton just got up to find a tree.

One single shot I heard
   and no one yelled, "Fire in the hole!"
   Clayton didn't hit the ground like he should have.
   "Get the fuck down, Clayton!"
   "Yes, sir!"
   The round went in his mouth, out the neck.
   Clayton hit the ground.

"Charlie - Charlie-2. 1 down.
   No medivac needed.
   Sniper, yes. OK. Out."
   I wonder, if Debbie Reynolds and
   Donald O'Connor were here,
   what they would have done.

No, I don't wonder that!
   What I really wonder is why that tree?
   or if he only took a shit, he'd be here now
   but he came late and left too early.

"Untitled"

Children. Ah! Children . . .
   What are they doing on this planet?
   To share our grief?
   To teach us to love?

What?
   God certainly let their presence be known in Viet Nam.
   A child was often a living bomb.
   I wonder what went through the mother's mind
   As her little girl walked up to the enemy
   And took her own life and others

   . . . Satisfaction?

Death is like an enema
  Only you hope
  it doesn't take that long.

It comes only once.

There is no
  "standing 'O'"

Cherries

Walking past the new guys,
   incoming and outgoing,
   it's all the same.

Either First Class or Transport,
   you will probably be in the right seat
   or the wrong bag.

I could read their faces
   and pick the ones
   that would be on the cargo manifest,
   sooner or later.

It didn't matter.
   When you're hamburg,
   who cares what the animal's name was.

Leaving Home

The saddest time in my life
    was hearing the thump of the landing gear
    pulling up in place
    and a slow, rolling 180 degree turn starboard
    with a view beyond description!

"My Bloody Battlegrounds." These were sacred!!
    My home, my soul,
    My friends are still there.

I'm lucky.
    I go back there every day.

And very often, at night, I wake suddenly,
    to a wall of red and white,
    screams of my men and my foe
    and I cannot stop
    or block them out.

In combat,
    where you die is where your soul remains.
    After all,
    that little plot is all you got.

Most Of The Way Home

When I made it to Boston, October 6,
  I wanted the next flight back
  to California - Hawaii - Vietnam.
  A little paperwork and then
  I'd surely be home -
  a little case of misinterpretation.
  I thought home was the U.S.
  I was never more wrong.

Seventeen years haven't passed.
  Seventeen minutes, maybe.
  I never came back.
  I got lost in between!

Even now, with a wonderful family,
  who loves me,
  I'm a sailor who needs the open seas,
  a professional soldier who needs a cause.
  That "cause" I turned my back to
  and it's on my mind,
  always.

These beautiful little faces look up at me,
  instant to instant.
  I want to pick them up, hug them,
  and on the other side of the coin,
  just squeeze the trigger.

Friends

Yes, I miss all those friends I had
   while in the Service.
   But most died right away.
   The rest are just waiting.

When we accepted our commission,
   we believed in the System
   because we were part of it.
   Thank God they couldn't see
   what would have happened to them,
   if they came back,
   wounded, broken, but alive.

They would rather have been
   with someone they could count on.
   At least the enemy
   you could meet face to face.

I Miss This

Rain so loud, drowning out the enemy fire.
   Rain so heavy that tears don't show.
   Rain so warm, so friendly, so beautiful
   your shivering fears disappear.
   Just RAIN.

It has no memory.
   It has no fear, no enemy.
   It has no needs, like me or you.

It captivates you.
   It brings back the days when Mom said,
   "You can't go out. You might catch cold."
   She loved me.

But here and now it's different.
   There is no Mom to say, "I love you. Don't go out."

Only death that waits until it stops raining.

I love the rain.
   Even now, when I see people run for shelter
   when it starts to pour,
   I look up and feel and remember
   when it meant warmth, protection.

Please, God, rain on me when I'm gone.
   I would like that.

Freedom Of The Press

I sit befuddled,
   half here, the rest locked up.
   The faces come and go
   as fast as the mind allows.
   It feeds me when I'm hungry
   and prepared.

I write down the happenings.
   Snap!
   A dastardly deed
   come and gone.
   All of it,
   except the aftermath.

I look at my losses
   and they add up
   to Fonda's flashing face.

The ambush on us
   would not have happened
   if we had not discussed our discontent
   over the actions of our families and friends
   being blinded by the press.

Evening news - Gospel!

National Guard

If you are a nice guy,
    you should be a father to your children,
    husband to the little woman,
    and a coach in the Little League,
    a town meeting member,
    play a little golf with the Jaycees,
    have a secure job,
    be a respectable citizen,
    registered voter, tax payer,
    member of every and all clubs
    you have the time to help.

But if your desires go beyond the simple life,
    beyond security, a little risky,
    a bigger challenge, a gamble,
    to put your life on the line
    where the loser loses ALL -
    and the winner keeps his life
    because he fought the odds and beat 'em.

Ever heard of the "Spirit of America?"
    I haven't heard those words
    or even read them since 1969,
    when my fellow 2LT's were dying with the SPIRIT.
    We loved America
    but whatever happened to our people?

We the people of the United States, if need be,
   will take your homeless,
   your huddled masses yearning to be free,
   give you that Freedom,
   keep all our promises
   and bear the burden of the wars.
   I challenge you America,
   to live up to that promise of President Lincoln.

We, the anguished, forgotten warriors,
   are calling for your hand,
   and, as always,
   we will keep our promises, our oaths,
   with our blood,
   and our last remaining breath
   to fight for "We, the People"
   our Country.

We the Veterans have never ever, ever let you down.
   In God's Name, I pray,
   Bless you, America!
   The time is now.

12:04 p.m.　　　Friday 13th, 1987
Who the hell do you think you are?!

I've been going to the Veterans Administration Hospital since 1975. I thought I had seen the worst cases of dejected, rejected, shit, shat, shot and all the rest. Take me - for years thinking only of Vietnam was "normal." I complained for years for any help, at least one warm bed for one cold vet, for one very sad, cold, lonely me! Poor me, poor me. Nobody cares. This kind of "shit."

Today, I was in the University of Michigan Hospital for ultraviolet rays for white blotches on my neck and face from trauma in Vietnam. I got sick while waiting for the shuttle back to the V.A. A van pulled up in front of me. This metallic slab dropped down and, a wheel chair, a small child weeping, not crying! But a haunting steady wail. The child was in serious pain most of the time. And she is dying. She goes there for treatments.

The wail - a constant sound that would not leave me alone the rest of the day and now I know I heard that sound before. I nailed it down to a place very far away.

"At their expense and our ignorance," we killed women and children. And the very same sound was there. We fired into the mass of bodies to stop the sounds. But the sound is with me always. As today - a reminder, in case I may forget!

Dear Lord, don't ever let me forget what was done in the name of Freedom. Don't slacken up! Give it to me with both barrels when I blame others for my "condition."

You let me live through impossible odds for something! Don't tell me what it is or was. Keep sending your love to my family, and to the little girl.

Thank you.

Dear Ike,

I was on your campus today. You probably wouldn't recognize it. It's huge, sprawling, winding over hills. They blended the old with the new so well.

MD, new, (He would've been seven years old when we were in country, Vietnam) the other day asked me if I was in the Korean or Vietnam Era War.

I truthfully said, "Civil War, North and South. Not my war but somebody else's."

I'm sorry you only lasted a month in 'Nam but it was best for you. It would have destroyed you to come back and see what and how Sam and the entire population treated us.

You and Becky were smart to take my advice and wait for the wedding till you came home.

You see, Ike, your heart was too fragile to survive the seventeen years I've put in. I often wonder what would have happened to you if we kicked you out of OCS. Your naivete about our government was etched on your tombstone the day you said, "So help me, God." - Our oath to Congress.

On Monday, I'm going to check around. And maybe meet with some old profs. Why? To tell them what you truly were made of. The kind, kindred spirit of a man - officer you were! That we were roomies while learning to kill the enemy with equipment made by the lowest bidder.

Especially to let them know you never found out what a fucked-up country did to you and all our Benning School For Boys, God rest their souls.

You were in the 90th percentile of the dying! Top of your class, as usual.

Bye, Ike.

My Old Home

The white delight
flying through
the open, broken side-door window

Just me and my '69 Spitfire
hoping for a sandwich
and some gasoline.

My old home, warm,
I picked it out.
At ten degrees,
I made the stairs with ease.

Mom opened the door.
"Hi, honey. How are you?
Hurry up, you'll freeze!"

"Dinner?" I politely asked.
She whispered,
"My Davie hasn't left yet."

"Her Davie!" My God, how that hurt!
He said I was a bum.
I constantly tried to explain
but even the doctors wouldn't listen.

I went back, slipping in my loafers
through two feet of the undelightful stuff and waited, and
waited,
and waited -
ten years to be just right.

My toes were icy blue
and his Mercedes ran on diesel.

Apparition

I remember, as a child,
   I asked God to help me become a priest,
   a good priest, a teacher.
   As I came to know more about life,
   I grew closer to God.
   Others grew away.

I went to mass sometimes three times a day.
   In any kind of weather.
   If I complained to myself,
   I would appologize
   and offer the pain up to God.

Silently, I pray now.
   I tell no one about how bad I feel.
   How serious the anguish is,
   the terror, terrors that I was placed with.
   There is no one that knows this feeling I have.
   (Except you.)

In your Name
   but when it came to face you
   with what I could call facing death,
   I would sum up all my feeling
   with your approval,
   and then go forth with all my plans
   as I saw fit,
   knowing that you were with me.

I can't believe this is coming from me on paper.
   This is the very first admission of your existance
   and assistance
   I ever made
   while engaged in a killing war.

Is there some explanation I can look for -
   I know you're still in touch with me.
   As I write this, you are looking at me
   from the cross.
   Did you give me a cross to carry through life?

You saved me for something.
   It is your way.
   Many times you were there.
   I could feel your strong support
   and with that, we saved others.

I never thanked you,
   and I never thanked me.
   I think, during a war, everyone believes.

December 24, 1969

We had set up an ambush site
overlooking a small fishing village.

We knew how many V.C. were hiding there
but the village was considered friendly,
so random fire or air strike was out.

A three or four year old girl came from the village.
She had a gift of death.
At ten feet, I saw what it was.
I fired right through her little body.
She was scrambled.

Later on, a woman came up the same hill, holding a baby
with the intestines dragging in the sand.
I stood up.

She threw the living baby on my boots.
She looked at the crying baby, then at me, then at my men,
said something in Vietnamese,
turned and walked back
to the village.
For all I know,
it could have been "Merry Christmas."
How nice.

This little event changed my life
I dropped to my knees, blessed myself,
threw my weapon down and said
at the top of my lungs, for the whole world,
"God forgive me!!!!!!!"

It's sixteen years later and I have a four year old daughter.
And every time I see her face,
I also see the face of the little one that I killed.
Even my two year old son is part of this constant exchange.

God hasn't forgiven me yet.
I'll wait. I'm a stubborn bastard.

Death with Honor.
   Made sense in 'Nam.
   Life back in the States,
   like Ham and Motherfuckers

From then on, you were scum.
   The V.A. wanted no part.
   Your family wanted you out.
   The friends you had -
   were had.

So you went
   to the only place of solitude,
   your subconscious,
   and got rejected.

The anguish was delightful.
   Pain, agony, guilt,
   and all the other feelings that you had
   were at least familiar.

So you called them friends.

Life Expectancy of a 2LT

"The closer you come to being killed, the stronger you become."
- Nitsche.

This bit of philosophy did nothing
    for all my deceased friends, roommates.
    Maybe, if I had told them
    before their arrival in Vietnam,
    they might have survived.

But my friends in OCS knew
    what the score was.
    It wouldn't have changed them
    even if they knew they would die.
    We had a special belief
    about Duty, Honor, Country.

I still do, but there are exceptions:
    Hanoi Jane, the media,
    and an uncaring public caused
    a lot of confusion and death.

The V.A. is doing its best
    to convince my children
    never to go to war for this country
    unless they dump the V.A.
    and start a caring system
    without budget on their minds.

I can't keep you alive, my son.
    The government said I was over budget.
    And all these pacemakers have to be returned
    before Fiscal '87.
    All those who had the V.A.
    handle the internment of your fathers
    must pay an additional fee
    or the marker will be removed.

"In God We Trust."

War is Hell?

War is not hell -
   because I've been in war
   and I've gone to hell.
   There's a very big difference.

War has challenge, excitement
   Fear turned into heroics.

Hell, on the other hand,
   is just plain crowded.

A New Definition

War is a twenty-four hour romance.
   Whether you love it or hate it,
   it can be both many times.

That's why we divorce it,
   to get rid of the memories
   all the while looking
   for the ultimate weapon.

Wow, aren't we something!
   We even erect images of ourselves
   to carry on with the carnage.

If you can come up with a better reason,
   you're a better man.
   But we always manage to forget
   the disabled veteran
   from the last war
   "Cost Prohibitive"

America's Abortion, 1975

I once had a heart that cared.
  Now, that heart is missing -
  Only numbness remains.

Who can understand
  what it's like to lose
  two hundred and forty friends
  in little more than one year?

Those lives were quickly taken,
  one at a time.
  The loss I cannot feel.

Those friends were the lives
  inside the hearts and minds
  of over two hundred men
  who felt the need to defend
  against aggression
  to the end.

At home, they had no friends.
  We all were becoming
  America's abortion.

What does this do to a man
  still alive,
  knowing he's the last
  to survive?

When is it appropriate
  to put all the emotions
  back inside
  and face the inevitable?

Another Mortal Sin

I'll bet you didn't know this.
  The highest rate of men
  who wanted to stay another year or so
  were the combat soldiers.

This may be a bit of the Blarney
  but reason has it that soldiers,
  who have paid such a price
  want to stay and fight
  and see who wins.

All the other wars we were in
  they let us stay.
  But not this one.

The Child

As I listen to their happiness
   from a playful scream
   to singing a song
   that hasn't been written,

I try to lock them in my heart
   for safe keeping.

I will always carry with me
   the memories
   of dying children.

First, last, and always,
   Vietnam.

Why Now?

I went to a parade the papers called
   the biggest Chicago ever had.
   It was for the Vietnam Vets,
   by the Vietnam Vets.
   Now that's really hard to swallow,
   but it happened.

It should be in the "Guinness."
   The watchers were on lunch break.
   Others were stranded there
   because we blocked the traffic.
   Some came honestly.

It was the most guilt-ridden parade ever viewed.
   Those who came for the Vets' sake
   were family and friends
   and they were the worst offenders.
   Why didn't they do something
   ten years ago?
   Great friends.

Late This Afternoon

The chair I live, sleep, and write in
   became too difficult to sit in.
   I found myself too comfortable.
   I decided to lie on the floor,
   covered with log cabin toys and many others.
   I fell into a depressive sleep.
   (I had not taken my meds.)

I sprawled across the toys
   with a poncho liner on me
   and felt totally uncomfortable
   just like Vietnam - an ambush!

My visitor came to me without delay - Flash!
   He took over my being.
   Then it was I,
   with all the feelings of war, of sin.

That's a good one, sin.
   A newcomer? Can't be.
   We were born with original sin,
   and left totally alone
   to commit more!

God told us not to do those Special 10,
   so we did and, baby, look at us now.

We go to war
   "In God We Trust."
   We blame others for our shortcomings
   or call even the devil to blame.

We even turn the other (noble) cheek
   for an easier out!
   Even the Almighty Buck stops here.

On Earth, we try -
   our guilty, our power, our patience,
   to climb the tallest, see the smallest,
   to build the best,
   but we never try hard enough
   to stop hunger, murder, war,
   ourselves from promoting the defiance
   of the Special 10
   that we were given as a guide to avoid,
   not a law to break.

Will we ever change?
   I'm asking me. My answer: No!
   There is no "why" to this question!
   Only forgive and forget - the Grand Denial!
   And we are very good at it.
   We hire people to listen and forgive.
   And we buy our way out of trouble
   with thirty pieces of silver.
   We kill our last hope of anything
   that is good and just
   "In God's Name."

What Else Is New

I suppose you know by now
   that Vietnam has never left me alone.
   It never will, I know.

Feel the breeze.
   It will tell you
   by the way it shocks your senses.

Burning chills,
   the smell of tinged hair,
   rancid body parts
   only hours old.

It's wet from blood.
   It's dry from the searing heat
   produced by the velocity
   of the spent round
   past your ears.

Now do you understand?
   Have you been here before?

Every day I see
   the faces of those I've killed
   and their children.
   And now I see the faces
   of those children
   I didn't kill.

We all make mistakes.

Title, Optional

I occasionally wear my Army fatigues,
   (It makes me feel good inside, a pro.)
   and leave them on when I sleep -
   added familiarity, protection.
   Sometimes I wear them to the store.

"Are you in the National Guard?"
   I reply, "sort of."
   Then I say, "S.F."
   They look puzzled.
   Then, I put on my beret
   and say again, "S.F.!" "Green Beret?"

"Oh . . . I thought that was just a movie!"
   "Nope!"
   I hop in the car and drive away -
   empty.

I forgive these people.
   I don't forgive their parents.
   The longest, "lost" war in our history
   and their parents, teachers and publishers
   never told them the truth.

"Kids, we didn't care about "them."
   We had our own problems
   at home and in school.
   It was really hard
   to avoid the Draft."

I really get pissed.

Yes It Could

Could it be
   that the people back home
   who hated us
   were actually acting out
   their own aggression
   in a war that we had no presence being in.

And above all,
   it lasted one generation
   and cost a bundle.

And now the hidden truth -
   We were coming home
   in drips and drabs
   from a war that was still going on,
   and we were holding the bag of lost causes
   and the supreme cause
   of their discontent.

I think this needs no supporting evidence.
   Just look at what you did to them
   And where they are today.

God bless them one and all.

Give and Take

When Megan, my first and only daughter, was born,
I saw her before Mom.
"Oh, boy! It's a girl!"
I was happy.
And then, all my thoughts went back
to Vietnam.

One face after another,
some bodies mutilated beyond sex.
The ones I killed via the Air Force and Navy
didn't get to me as much
as the ones who looked deeply into my eyes
and sadly wondered,
as though to ask me,
"Are you going to kill me now?"

Seeing my daughter come to life,
crying for Mom, etc.
I felt the guilt.
God, how can you give me this miracle
and let me take others away?

I am happy for Megan and Danny to be alive
and not too sure about me.
I can never be close to them.
The other faces are in the way.
I am the saddest today.

PTSD vs. Wife #1
1974

The room is empty -
   the TV on the floor,
   upstairs empty.

Suits in a pile,
   no hangers,
   no soap.

Knife, fork, spoon,
   no food,
   no note.

A chair in the livingroom.
   I wish it was plugged in.

The Old - The New

I

If you could understand
   in my past, pre-Vietnam
   all things I held in high esteem -
   love, family, friends, relatives,
   kites, boats, babies, mothers - anyone's,
   all people,
   respect of my accomplishments, by myself,
   Never ever low esteem then.

I was the best.
   I played with everyone, did everything.
   People were my friends.
   Everything was just fantastic
   through my eyes.
   A survivor! - even as a child.

These are not even in my thoughts anymore
   and, yes, I do this to myself.
   I can't stop it.
   I was a happy person.

Now comes Charlie-2,
   beaten but not out, kicked but not down,
   hurt beyond reason,
   but still has a spot in his heart
   for someone who hurts a little more.

II

Success is measured by one's own eyes
  and the distance they see,
  forever.

III

They said it couldn't be done!
  and they were right -
  we all died trying,
  my commissioning class, over two hundred.
  That should teach us all a lesson.

But will our sons feel this way
  when they read our history -
  the true history, written in blood!

If they're anything like us,
  even just a little,
  watch out world!
  The Sons of Liberty are ready.
  They will soon be upon you!
  The ones who denied us a victory
  know who you are!

For Them

When I was very young,
  I had metal soldiers.
  We played, a winning side.

Sure we had losses
  but we had resupply
  in my shoebox,
  and food was not a problem.

When I was not very young,
  a 21 year old LT.,
  we played the winning side,
  but our supply of troops
  was limited.

The food was fine,
  when it came.
  The water was green,
  supplied by bomb craters.

When I came back to the U.S.,
  in 1970, October,
  at the airport,
  6 a.m. EST, Boston.
  Only a handful of soldiers were there
  afraid to call "home" for a ride.

They were afraid that the response
  would be universal
  "baby killer", etc.
  Seventeen years later,
  it still hasn't changed.

They just wrote it off -
  a one-page reference to Viet Nam.
  I read it in a history book.

Don't Blame Me

Two gooks were parked
   in a spot for handicapped parking.
   Their license plate
   was not in keeping with the law.

I wanted to kill them
   but I had ice cream in my bag.

Just A Thought

I grew up in a country without war
   and sometimes peace,
    So I don't know what it is like to grow up
    in a country at war for 100-plus years.

So, let's give these Vietnamese
   a chance to prosper and grow.
   We all - every generation here -
   were immigrants at one time.

But as I show my concern,
   I'll kill the fucking bastards
   who took over two hundred friends
   from me.

I'll cut their hairless balls off for display
   and put a frag in their lunch pail.

Today,
　my Megan and I
　"talked"
　for "a minute"
　to each other!

It was the longest time
　that I can recall.

She is five and a half.

Survivor - One Heartbeat Away

To be a survivor
  Don't turn your back.

None of those people
  who I call "they"
  would like to be reminded
  by a survivor
  that "they" lost one
  and we didn't.

The ground you walk on is very sacred
  to them!
  You stand for all that is not holy.
  (You are bad. Evil.)

The good die young
  "Theirs."

The sad part,
  You believe them.

Guilt

Deep red thoughts
   enter my soul always.
   It was pure white,
   long ago!

"Am I next?"
   said the last alive child.
   "Yes," I said.
   And it was done!
   or was it just a reflection
   of you

In your twenties
   from a pool of blood
   Not realizing then,
   it would blacken
   your soul
   when it dried.
   And made permanent.

Twilight Zone

When I make it
  To the point of no return -
  Five minutes to Eternity exit
  Next right, Vietnam

I'll look back
  At my memories
  And I'll try to see
  The things that made memories
  So wonderful.

But all I'll see
    Is a
        very
            ugly
                scar.

Sooner The Better

You now have the most difficult chore ahead
    and you can't explain why this distance you created
    is so great.

Children that you killed
    the same age as your own
    May God forgive you.

It's tough
    when they stop saying
    "Good night, Daddy. I love you."

"You're no fun." "Why does Daddy hide?"
    "I want to play with my friends."
    The list goes on.

Look deep inside, Fella.
    You are now paying the entry fee
    for the right to live.
    The Title Match is yet to come.

I entered this war
   with all the training
   I would ever need.
   But as they say
   in a professional way,
   you gotta pay the piper.

"These first, hardest years
   are going to make or break you."
   In the Arts, you gotta pay,
   and hope it pays off.

I trained, I learned, I won,
   I was a hero, living legend,
   then I realized that I had the right
   to choose from the beginning,

But I still had to pick up the tab,
   clear the tables, and wait on others

And, after seventeen years,
   I'm still paying for that damn right
   to choose the after dinner wine.

Last Request

I want a farm—
   One acre per battle fought,
   One each a wildflower,
   For all the memories.

A tribute living silently
   On a gentle slope,
   Sharing beauty every day.
   In love with life
            . . . at last.

About Post-traumatic Stress Disorder (PTSD)

Post-traumatic Stress Disorder has been under study for many years and it will likely be for many more before it is fully understood, if ever As yet, no one knows why some people suffer from it and others don't, even though they went through similar situations.

After a traumatic event, some people may experience emotional numbing, a blocking out of the strong emotions associated with the event. This period may last days, weeks, months or, as in most cases, years. Then, they may begin to experience stress-related problems such as the ones listed below. They may distance themselves from others for fear of losing people they care about. They have nightmares and flash backs - the mind's way of trying to re-experience the stressful event, to deal with it and master it, so that it is no longer a disaster which is emotionally overwhelming.

Some symptoms of Post-traumatic Stress Disorder are: Depression, suicidal feelings, thoughts, anger, rage, retaliation, violence, emotional numbing, memory impairment, sleep disturbances, survivor guilt, emotional suicide, problems with intimate relationships, fear of losing loved ones, difficulty making emotional commitments, emotional distance from wife, family, etc., cynicism, distrust, alienation from society, sensitivity to justice, anxiety, hypertension, alcoholism, drug use, distrust of government, flashbacks to 'Nam, fantasies of violence, self-deceiving and/or self-punishing behavior, instability at work, family life, etc., loss of interest in work, people, or self, avoidance of activities with memory of war trauma, and when under stress, a tendency to react with violence.

Statistics concerning Vietnam vets are disturbing. Over one million Vietnam veterans suffer from PTSD in varying degrees. An eight year study by the Vietnam Era Research Project, on combat vets, found that 40% of them were unemployed and 1 out of 3 had "re-adjustment problems serious enough to impair their functioning." Vietnam vets have a significantly higher rate of divorce, unemployment, and suicide (100,000 – government figures) than their non-veteran peers. With more public awareness and funding for counselling and research, more Vietnam veterans can be helped.

It wasn't until 1980, that the VA and the medical community recognized that Vietnam veterans needed specialized treatment to help them cope with the Vietnam experience. Now, some vets are working through their problems with the help of spouses, friends, other Vietnam vets, and professional therapists. The storefront Vet Centers have been especially helpful to vets, with their Outreach Program, rap sessions, and counselling of vets and their families. (We don't understand why the VA wants to close them down.)

If you are a veteran having trouble with your Vietnam experience, help is available! We urge you to get help, for without proper treatment, PTSD only gets worse. Please contact your local Vet Center, veterans' organization, or the VA, as soon as possible.